T H E   B E S T I N

LOBBY DESIGN

HOTELS & OFFICES

ALAN PHILLIPS

ROTOVISION

A QUARTO BOOK

Published by ROTOVISION SA
Route Suisse 9
CH-1295 Mies
Switzerland

Distributed to the trade in the
United States & Canada by
Watson-Guptill Publications
1515 Broadway
New York, NY 10036

ISBN 0-8230-6136-1

This book was designed and produced by
Quarto Publishing plc
6 Blundell Street
London N7 9BH

Creative Director: Terry Jeavons
Designer: Wayne Blades
Editor: Viv Croot

Typeset in Great Britain by
Central Southern Typesetters, Eastbourne
Manufactured in Hong Kong by Excel Graphic Arts Ltd
Printed in Hong Kong by Leefung-Asco Printers Ltd

Contents

Introduction 6

Traditional 18

Modern 54

New Modern 174

Interventionist 196

Index of Projects 222

Directory of Practising Architects 223

Photographic Acknowledgements 224

Introduction

Introduction

The lobby or entrance place is that part of a building that greets the visitor and user; it is therefore the place in which the architecture can first declare itself, providing a part of the whole as a sample of the quality of the rest. The entrance place offers the architect an opportunity to design a paradigm of the spirit and language of the whole building; the lobby becomes the essence of the architectural intention by condensing aesthetic ambitions into one primary public space.

The Lloyds Building, London, England
The huge, heroic atrium at once dominates and distinguishes the building dubbed by critics 'the cathedral of work'.
ARCHITECT: Richard Rogers Partnership Ltd, London, England

Die Staatsgalerie, Stuttgart, Germany
The lobby is characterized by a gleaming and glazed serpentine wall that embraces the reception area and gives way to a lift structure which, by revealing its structure and mechanism, establishes a bridge between the architecture of the museum and the art it contains.
ARCHITECT: Stirling, Wilford & Associates, London, England

The Riverside Centre, Brisbane, NSW, Australia
Exquisite detail, the meticulous assembly of
materials and colour and cleverly orchestrated
artificial lighting create a welcoming atmosphere
in what otherwise may seem an overwhelmingly
imposing space.
ARCHITECT : Harry Seidler and Associates,
Milson's Point, NSW, Australia

Function and Philosophy   Entrance spaces, especially those to corporate and municipal buildings, are often large in scale. In addition to comfort and function, the lobby will symbolize the activities and qualities of the building's user. Through architecture, the client can express an attitude to the public about the building's function and their company principles and philosophies. In one often heroic space, the lobby will expose the personality of the building's function. At the same time, and by way of underlining an expression of function, the architect will also be declaring a personal manifesto. The marriage of the client and the architect will often be made because the ambitions of both are compatible and mutually reinforcing.

The Lobby as Information Centre   The lobby is also required to reveal the building's geography. Like the atrium to a classical Roman villa, from where the visitor could find staircases and entrances leading to other areas of the house, the lobby is responsible for the clear presentation of information about the building's physical organization. In addition to the reception desk, the entrance will reveal vertical circulation systems, architectural hierarchies together with public and private spaces as well as rest areas.

In large municipal buildings or hotels the lobby has much work to do. If the first and primary space confuses the visitor and fails to guide and direct coherently, enjoyment for the rest of the building will decrease. The most successful lobbies are those that do not need to rely on signage and graphic devices but establish route, circulation and function by architectural articulation, language, materials and form.

Bank of China, Hong Kong
The principal lobby space is distinguished by its huge scale and the interrelationship of two opposing geometries.
ARCHITECT: Pei Cobb Freed & Partners, New York City, New York, USA

The Lobby as Refuge   In dense urban areas, the lobby is often seen as a refuge. The entrance place is translated as an urban oasis, somewhere to escape the noise and aggression of the outside world. The formal device of capturing a rural landscape in an urban area has been used to great effect. The surreal juxtaposition of enclosed forest and city skyscraper establishes an architectural philanthropy which serves to enhance the reputation of the building. Other formal devices, including the use of water, tents, artworks and kinetics, seek to provide similar circumstances. In different contexts, the lobby might rely on counterpoint to express

Battery Park Financial Center, New York City, New York, USA
The huge lobby is an extreme example of the urban refuge. A glazed arcade provides shelter and climate control to a captured landscape of palms within the heartland of downtown New York.
ARCHITECT: Cesar Pelli Associates, New Haven, Connecticut, USA

Stockley Park, Heathrow, London, England
The structural concept is a development of the central 'Y' shaped element of two adjacent pitched roof enclosures. It has the advantages of better daylight penetration via rooflights located along the ridge thus separating them from drainage and avoiding complex waterproofing details. The east and west elevations are made up of double glazed units of which the internal face is stove enamelled with a white dot, varying in concentration from almost opaque at floor and eaves level to clear between desk top and eye level to reduce solar gain.
ARCHITECT: Foster Associates, London, England

a specificity of function, where the visitor will experience an almost abstract world to that outside the entrance door. In hot climates, the device of establishing the lobby as a type of benign harbour will be reinforced through carefully organized climate control systems. Even in the most modest of spaces, a cool hall offered as a retreat from a hot and humid city will be interpreted as a mark of success.

It is when the circumstances of climate, context, form, materials and structure are brought together through scale, composition and proportion that the great lobbies are made. With improved knowledge of the behaviour of heating and cooling systems and of the contribution of passive energy, lobbies are now often expressed as organizing voids that extend the full height of the building. The atrium system allows for experiment in scale and proportion as well as providing dynamic lighting orchestrations.

Precedent and the Future   The present is a mirror of the past. To congratulate a contemporary building is to honour its precedent. Accordingly, it is necessary to place today's architecture into a cultural context as well as a physical one. The first half of the twentieth century saw the work of some extraordinary masters including Mendelsohn, Aalto, Le Corbusier, Jacobsen and Scharoun from a huge family of great European architects, together with Mies van der Rohe, Louis Kahn and Frank Lloyd Wright working in America and building around the world. Their wealth of influence through innovation, invention and revolution linked to radical manifestos proclaiming ideologies, theories and philosophies have touched every corner of late twentieth-century architecture.

Finlandia Hall, Helsinki, Finland
The Finlandia Hall was completed in 1971. It is a great essay in circulation and foyer design with the principal, secondary and tertiary spaces all being fed effortlessly from the major space that is marked by structure and the footprint of the building plan above.
ARCHITECT: Alvar Aalto

**Mineworker's Union Building, Berlin,
Germany**
The geometry of the mineworker's building is
reinforced with a close attention to detail and an
engaging manipulation of scale and proportion,
brought together in light, space and
composition.
ARCHITECT: Eric Mendelssohn

The Jewish Community Center, Trenton, New Jersey, USA

The Jewish Center, built between 1955 and 1956, develops a hierarchy of void within a central space bathhouse temple and leads the eye to a type of occulus. A precisely engineered geometry and an understanding of light allows the building to achieve great presence from modest materials.

ARCHITECT: Louis Kahn

Many of the entrance spaces bear the mark of those early ideas. Sometimes they remain as an organizing principle or philosophical ordering system. In many buildings, the language of Modernism is expressed idiomatically but developed through contemporary refinements of the enabling technologies. In some, the manifestos are translated polemically and principles are deliberately counteracted to set up a new radicalism.

The best examples of lobby design are the product of innovative support from enlightened clients who believe that the end of the twentieth century, in common with the closing of all previous centuries, should have an architecture appropriate and contemporary to its time, culture, context and civilization.

Aarhus Town Hall, Aarhus, Denmark
Although built between 1936 and 1942, the foyer to Arne Jacobson's Town Hall, with its glazed screen at one end, has been a formative influence in the development of central atria during the latter part of the century.
ARCHITECT: Arne Jacobson & E. Moller

Traditional   Architecture and culture

cannot be separated. Neither is it possible for a nation's culture to develop without respect for and reference to the past. Accordingly, if an architecture has evolved from a cradle of traditional cultural values, it will reflect an historical language contemporary with the point at which these values were recognized. In some instances, especially when a new use is proposed for an historically fragile building, facsimiles of the traditional language can support the existing architectural grammar to reassert the cultural value. There is an integrity to this approach.

Recently, however, many new buildings have been made comprising fragments and sometimes entire ensembles that belong to a recognized tradition but of another age and another culture. In addition to this type of anachronistic quotation, there is a renewed interest in decoration, ornament and appliqué, as well as metaphor and symbol, as a means of securing another layer of complexity. At the extreme, some architects are asking, for example, that a traditional Greek device hold court in a twentieth-century office building lobby in downtown New York.

If there is a match between object and subject, with scholarship as the ultimate arbiter of taste, then this form of architectural expression can sometimes be successful. If scholarship is absent and traditional languages are decontextualized, then wilfulness can only parody the original architecture.

18

The orthodox and academic view of the application of a traditional architectural language for late twentieth-century buildings is represented in the lobbies of Skidmore, Owings & Merrill, among others. Where historical and cultural accuracy is deliberately ignored in the cause of wit, allegory and comedy, as illustrated in Michael Graves' work for Disney, a hybrid style has evolved, reminiscent of the rampant borrowings of the Victorians. History will decide whether this type of architectural eclecticism has any value or, value apart, what role it will play in the development of our architectural heritage.

Banque Bruxelles Lambert, Milan Italy
To intensify the counterpoint between the new architectural design and the original architecture, the simple device of cordoning the new areas with a conceptual black line was employed to help define the edges where new meets old. The line appears in various forms: in the entrance's grand staircase, the black floor lamps and in other forms throughout the building.
ARCHITECT: Emilio Ambasz & Associates, New York City, New York, USA

BUPA Hospital, Leicester, England
The brief was to create a new corporate interior
design scheme for the hospitals and medical
centres run by BUPA, a private healthcare
company. The scheme, which reinforces the
desired '4-star hotel' image while at the same
tiem creating a relaxed, professional and caring
ambience, is to be implemented throughout the
BUPA services.
ARCHITECT: McColl, London, England

AT & T, Chicago, Illinois, USA

This building is characterized principally by the elegance of its proportions. Natural and artificial light animate the lobby space via the reflectivity of highly polished floor and wall surfaces.

ARCHITECT: Skidmore Owings & Merrill, New York City, New York, USA

757 Third Avenue, New York City, New York, USA

The central rotunda is marked by the floorscape, comprising two interlocking squares of polished stone that point to the corridor spaces and a circle of columns that support upper galleries.

ARCHITECT: Skidmore, Owings & Merrill, New York City, New York, USA

Cook-Fort Worth Children's Medical Center, Fort Worth, Texas, USA

The atmosphere in this lobby is friendly and imaginative. The central atrium, which serves as the building's main lobby, is a child's vision of the inner courtyard of an enchanted castle rendered in soft coloured hues. The three lower levels are a composition of features which rise to towers in each corner.

ARCHITECT: David M. Schwarz Architectural Services, Washington D.C., USA

Epworth House Securities, London, England
The circular columns, curved reception desk and
restored lightwell provide the composition of
soft lines, in contrast to the simple use of
materials and monochromatic paintwork.
ARCHITECT: McColl, London, England

Bond Street House, London, England
Bond Street House was originally built around 1800. The main reception area to the offices uses traditional material and contemporary geometries to create a new interior that is respectful to the past and faithful to the present. Low-voltage quartz halogen lights provide task lighting, with ambient lighting established by recessed fixtures set into a cut in the ceiling.
ARCHITECT: McColl, London, England

27

Walt Disney World Swan Hotel, Lake Buena Vista, Florida, USA

The Swan Hotel is oriented to the crescent shaped lake shared by its companion hotel, the Dolphin. It is organized around a landscaped courtyard defined by two projecting wings of guestrooms. An octagonal lobby in the center of the courtyard connects the hotel restaurants and facilities to the causeway that crosses the lake to the Dolphin. The entrance foyer has a tented ceiling and columns resembling bundles of palm reeds (a suitable swan habitat); the main lobby contains a central fountain and a floral pattern on its walls and vaulted ceiling.

ARCHITECT: Michael Graves, Princeton, New Jersey, USA

Walt Disney World Swan Hotel continued over page

Cour des Loges Hotel, Lyon, France
Cour des Loges, in the centre of old Lyon, is a result of the integration of four adjoining protected buildings, dating from the fourteenth to the seventeenth centuries. Renovated renaissance galleries, original beamed ceilings, mullioned windows and outdoor gardens are all capped by a glass domed ceiling to conjure an internal lobby from what was once an exterior court.
ARCHITECT: Yves Bouchatat and Pierre Vurpas with Jean-Luc and Hélène Matthias for the Cour des Loges Hotel, Lyon, France

222 North Lasalle, Chicago, Illinois, USA
The lobby, surrounded by arched headed
decorated openings and capped by an
illuminated ceiling, provides a rich and heroic
space within a building of great scale and
proportion.
ARCHITECT: Skidmore, Owings & Merrill,
Chicago, Illinois, USA

Windsor House, London, England

The prestigious Windsor House, opulently refurbished for the Norwich Union insurance group; classical use of symmetry and proportion is interpreted in a contemporary fashion. Behind the wide expanse of glass frontage, the lobby is protected by a row of top-lit columns, lavish sentinels marshalled behind the diminutive reception desk.

ARCHITECT: McColl, London, England

**Residential Lobby, 132 East Delaware Place,
Chicago, Illinois, USA**
Symmetry contains this composition of
traditional and classical elements. Lighting is
effectively reflected from the ceilings with
fittings reinforcing the symmetrical
arrangement.
ARCHITECT: Pedersohn, Kohn, Fox & Connor,
Chicago, Illinois, USA

Sheraton Hotel, Brussels Airport, Brussels, Belgium
The Brussels Airport Sheraton Hotel lobby and foyer are heroic and monumental in scale. The softly tailored interiors are in contrast to the external steel and glass supporting assemblies.
ARCHITECT: ITT Sheraton, Brussels, Belgium

Sonesta Beach Hotel, Florida, USA
Colour, pattern, texture and light combine to give a painterly atmosphere to this hotel lobby.
ARCHITECT: McColl, London, England

**Regent Beverly Wilshire, Hollywood,
California, USA**

Huge mirrored walls and a polished stone floor
reflect this revivalist interior. This grand lobby is
part of a complete renovation of the hotel,
transforming the original 1920s building into a
prestigious European style hotel.

ARCHITECT: Project Associates, Los
Angeles, California, USA

Four Seasons Hotel, Toronto, Ontario, Canada

Quiet opulence is achieved in this hotel lobby by the use of colour and materials, particularly the Quebec mahogany granite floor, boldly bordered in *nero assoluto* granite with ivory accent design. The floor's intricate patterning recalls luxurious old-world English and French hotels built when first class travel was the private claim of the privileged and the few. Carpets, ceiling and floors repeat an oval pattern to soften the grid of the rectangular marble columns.

ARCHITECT: Four Seasons Hotels and Rosalie Wise Design Incorporated, Toronto, Ontario, Canada

Washington Square, Chicago, Illinois, USA
The Washington Square project is a conversion
of an antiquated warehouse into a first class
office building. A colonnade of stone and lighted
glass block columns mark the entry. Passing
through the cross axis of a skylit galleria
demarcating old and new, the visitor ascends to
the centralized lobby. The composition of a
masonry stone, terrazzo, brass and glass
presents historical familiarity and yet enticing
surprises. Masonry is the key material in unifying
old and new and providing warmth and texture.
ARCHITECT: Pappageorge Haymes,
Chicago, Illinois, USA

1133 Connecticut Avenue N.W., Washington D.C., USA

This building, also known as 'Raleigh's' building after the store which comprises the street level, with offices above. The office lobby is defined by a limestone bracket supported pediment over a two-storey arched opening. A glass and metal canopy lends emphasis and an air of tradition. Under it, a granite paving pattern begins in the sidewalk and flows into the building. Granite, limestone and brass are used in more intimate areas of the lobby. Upper portions are built in colour matched brick and pre-cast concrete. Timber furniture is richly decorated in marquetry to provide a counterpoint to the harder background surfaces.

ARCHITECT: David M. Schwarz Architectural Services, Washington DC, USA

Metropolitan Square, St Louis, Missouri, USA
Metropolitan Square, a 42-storey luxury office block is the tallest building in St Louis. To encourage public access and usage, a pedestrian arcade encircles the building with its ground level completely devoted to public spaces. A huge glass clad atrium leads to an interior lobby rimmed by restaurants and shops. Rich finishes are used throughout. The lobby is formally and symmetrically composed, using traditional materials and a light, strong floor pattern to reflect the glazed ceiling. The walls and columns are of marble and the floor is paved with marble and granite arranged in a hexagonal pattern that is the building's trademark. Brass fixtures and trims add to the feeling of elegance.
ARCHITECT : Hellmuth Obata & Kassabaum, Inc., St Louis, Missouri, USA

**Crown American Corporate Office Building,
Johnston, Pennsylvania, USA**
The Crown building is a four-storey structure
organized round a central atrium which rises
through the entire building, unifying the interior.
The lobby is marked out in blues, pinks and
creams, all typical of the Graves palette. Artificial
lighting is largely concealed to wash the walls
and ceilings, with spotlighting over paintings
and furniture arrangements.
ARCHITECT: Michael Graves, Princeton,
New Jersey, USA

Lansdowne House, London, England

Lansdowne House is a listed 1930s building, originally designed as an apartment block, but now transformed into an office block. In the atrium, large clumps of mature bamboo tower up to an inverted glazed canopy, and their delicate leafy tops offer a pleasing contrast to the strong architectural style and highly polished finish of the atrium space. The stone-clad surrounding walls and floor reflect the light from above and work in counterpoint to the soft foliage.

ARCHITECT: Chapman Taylor Partners, London, England

Walt Disney World Dolphin Hotel, Lake Buena Vista, Florida, USA

The Dolphin Hotel faces its companion, the Swan Hotel across a large crescent shaped lake and a covered causeway connects the two hotel lobbies. The large vaulted entrance foyer of the Dolphin, flanked by grottos with running water, leads to a tented octagonal lobby with a central fountain. The Dolphin Hotel is full of reference, metaphor and symbolism which could be appropriate to the make-believe world of Disney and the self-declared Disney programme for 'entertainment architecture'.

ARCHITECT: Michael Graves, Princeton, New Jersey, USA

The Grand Hyatt Hotel, Hong Kong
The blue dished ceiling appears to float above two rows of illuminated columns. Reflections increase the perceived depth of the central space.
ARCHITECT: Hirsch/Bedner Associates, Santa Monica, California, USA

Four Seasons Hotel, Chicago, Illinois, USA
The main lobby is a luxurious expanse of
gleaming inlaid marble, interspersed with deep
pile carpets. The baroque interior sparkles with
an eccentric collection of chandeliers, furniture,
and plants sitting over a marbled floor all downlit
from the relatively simple ceiling system. At one
end of the lobby, a grand staircase sweeps up
dramatically to the ballroom on the next floor. In
another corner, an enormous white marble
fountain signals the entrance to the dining
facilities.
ARCHITECT: Four Seasons Hotels and Frank
Nicholson Incorporated, Concord,
Massachusetts, USA

The Humana Building, Louisville, Kentucky, USA

The Humana Building was designed as the corporate headquarters for a company specializing in healthcare. Within the outdoor loggia, which acts as the entrance to the building, a large waterfall fountain refers to the nearby falls of the Ohio River. Inside the building, the lobby is a sequence of spaces that rotates around a central rotunda which appears to be carved from a solid block of marble. This centrepiece generates the floor patterning that radiates toward the marble-clad walls which in turn rise from a highly decorated floor.

ARCHITECT: Michael Graves, Princeton, New Jersey, USA

▼

▼

▼

Modern

The word modern is confusing: applied to architecture, it implies a connection, however remote, with the philosophy of the Modern movement. Modernism was a revolution in architectural thought and expression, motivated as much by reaction to the eclecticism of nineteenth-century Revivalism as by a passionate ambition to develop a new architectural vocabulary that could promote social, political, cultural and philosophical reform.

It is as hard to define Modernism as it is easy to misunderstand it. What is clear is that clients in both private and public sectors see a modern architecture as a more appropriate response to the commercial and municipal worlds of the twentieth century than a recycled, misquoted, historical style whose unimaginative image is so often seen as the enemy of progress and the death of originality.

Modern architecture embraces new technologies. Through an honest expression of structure, form and fabric, modern architecture proclaims a truthfulness to function that by careful arrangement can create great and poetic spaces.

Modern architects direct the management and transformation of these technological systems towards a universal application, whether to provide a research facility for Schlumberger at Cambridge in England, an office tower in Tokyo by Norman Foster, or I. M. Pei's JFK Library in Boston, USA.

Battery Park Financial Center, New York City, New York, USA

This huge glazed atrium shelters a world within a world; the offices sit inside the envelope of the atrium, which also provides a year-round garden and a climatically stable urban refuge for the local community.

ARCHITECT: Cesar Pelli Associates, New Haven, Connecticut, USA

Canada Life Place, Potter's Bar, Hertfordshire, England

The floors of the Canada Life building are united by a full-height conservatory on the diagonal of the square plan, forming the heart and hub of the building. All circulation routes relate to this conservatory; planted balconies to the office floors have full-height glazing allowing views from the desks to the countryside beyond; at the ground level reception, visitors pass through a double-height cutaway corner and a lobby into the dramatic volume of the conservatory.

ARCHITECT: Rock Townsend, London, England

Tsukuba Civic Centre, Tokyo, Japan
The principal lobby is marked out with a series of
powerful bands that provide a direction, rhythm
and scale to the tall central spaces. Lighting is
arranged to darken the ceiling in contrast to
many atria, where the central light space is
distinguished by a glazed canopy.
ARCHITECT: Arata Isozaki, Tokyo, Japan

County Court House, Santa Barbara, California, USA
William Mooser's Court House, built in 1929, established one of many principles concerning multi-volume central spaces and high-level lights that has influenced a whole range of contemporary buildings.
ARCHITECT: William Mooser & Co.

John Darling Shopping Mall, Eastleigh, Hampshire, England

The linear entrance space is part arcade, part garden, part conservatory with recollections of the great English orangeries. Planted walls provide privacy under a light, white glass and steel canopy.

ARCHITECT: Hampshire County Architects Department, Winchester, Hampshire, England

Technical College, Farnborough, Hampshire

The entrance is a link corridor greenhouse and vaulted arcade, recalling Victorian structures and English landscapes. However, the structural support system in tubular and rolled hollow section is contemporary, and links tradition to the function of the building.

ARCHITECT: Hampshire County Architects Department, Winchester, Hampshire, England

Police Training Centre, Netley, Hampshire, England

A simple yet elegant arrangement of structure, placed under glazed pyramidal rooflights provides a symmetrical envelope for the principal staircase of a modest training centre.

ARCHITECT: Hampshire County Architects Departments, Winchester, Hampshire, England

The Burrell Gallery, Glasgow, Scotland
The Burrell Collection is housed outside
Glasgow. The entrance to the North Gallery is
distinguished by the juxtaposition of an historic
dooway inscribed into a contemporary wall. The
architectural fragment is memorialized and
retains its dignity rather than becoming part of a
pastiche.
ARCHITECT: Barry Gasson, Glasgow, Scotland

La Grande Arche, Paris, France

The *al fresco* lobby is capped by a tensile
structure that spans the inhabited walls of the
Arche. The two vocabularies work in
juxtaposition to set up an intriguing aesthetic
counterpoint.

ARCHITECT: Otto von Spreckelson

The Schomerhaus, near Vienna, Austria

The atrium to the Schomerhaus is a delicate composition of rotunda, staircase and rooflights which provides a cool and passive environment at the heart of the building. The spaces are characterized by fabric and structure brought together in light, without the need for ornament or decoration.

ARCHITECT: Heinz Tesar, Vienna, Austria

The Schomerhaus continued

John F Kennedy Center, USA

A monumentality of scale and a proper concern for perspective creates an heroic internal foyer appropriate to the function of the Center.

ARCHITECT: Edward Durell Stone, Boston, Massachusetts

The Richard Feigen Gallery, New York City, New York, USA

The main gallery and entrance space is a poetic relationship of a principal void contained by simple planes in perspective and relieved through a huge undulating soffit. The drama of the space is created by what is left out rather than what is put in.

ARCHITECT: Hans Hollein in association with Peter Blake, Vienna, Austria

Schlumberger Research Centre, Cambridge, England

A lightweight tensile structure forms a translucent canopy over the central space. The multi-purpose foyer serves the functions of lobby, rest area and garden.

ARCHITECT: Michael Hopkins and Partners, London, England

Neue Pinakothek, Munich, Germany
The foyer to this modest building is finely
sculpted in natural materials to provide for a rich
homogeneity of form and light.
ARCHITECT: A F von Branca, Munich, Germany

The Arab World Institute Building, Paris, France

The principal entrance areas are characterized by the interrelationship of passive and active systems, comprising fairface concrete, gridded screens and latticed steelwork constructions, all of which create a dynamic and facetic impact through a clear expression of the building's function.

ARCHITECT: Jean Nouvel, Paris, France

The Louvre, Paris, France
The huge pyramid sitting over the new entrance to the Louvre Art Gallery is both simple and complex, passive and active. The ancient figure interpreted in steel and glass provides an intervention that toasts the past while celebrating the present.
ARCHITECT: Pei Cobb Freed & Partners, New York City, New York, USA

Museum of Modern Art, Frankfurt, Germany
The all-white building comprises a clarity of
expression which is marked by a ramp that rises
through the triple-volume lobby space. Internal
and external screens provide both a transparency
and a translucency that filters light across the
cubic geometries of the building's composition.
ARCHITECT: Richard Meier & Partners,
New York City, New York, USA

The High Museum of Art, Atlanta, Georgia, USA

The principal spaces are articulated by a central rotunda and circulation ramp system leading to a series of galleries. The separation of structure and building envelope provides for both a visual layering and an ordering system for the principal public spaces.

ARCHITECT: Richard Meier & Partners, New York City, New York, USA

**British Petroleum National Headquarters,
Hemel Hempstead, Hertfordshire, England**
The central atrium is marked by a pair of lifts
whose skeletal support systems appear as two
enormous columns supporting the glazed roof
over. Galleries give way to office decks, all of
which have a transparency which exposes the
geography of the building.
ARCHITECT: Renton Howard Wood Levine
London, England

Die Staatsgalerie, Stuttgart, Germany
The principal reception area to the Art Gallery
sees set pieces such as monumental columns
and skeletal lift constructions sitting on an
artificial green landscape enclosed by a curved
skin of glass and steel.
ARCHITECT: Stirling, Wilford & Associates,
London, England

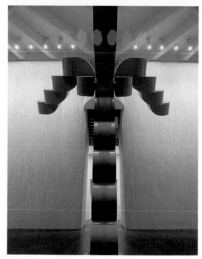

Riverside Centre, Brisbane, NSW, Australia
Close attention to detail and careful use of
artificial light confers an intimacy on the huge
proportions of the principal lobby of the
Riverside Centre. Much of the internal space is
animated by the canopy of geometric structural
patterns.
ARCHITECT: Harry Seidler and Associates,
Milson's Point, NSW, Australia

Shell Building, Melbourne, Victoria, Australia
At night, the principal lobby to the Shell Building
achieves its greatest drama by the orchestration
of artificial light to floors, ceilings and walls.
ARCHITECT: Harry Seidler and Associates,
Milson's Point, NSW, Australia

Capita Centre, Sydney, NSW, Australia
Orientation and a precise understanding of climate allows the geometry of this lobby and atrium space to take advantage of daylight and sunlight to animate the internal spaces.
ARCHITECT: Harry Seidler and Associates, Milson's Point, NSW, Australia

Security Pacific Hoare Govett Building, London, England

The central atrium space is carefully lit and beautifully detailed to provide a scenario for the internal landscape floor. Above ground floor level, a series of gridded screens and light steel frames create a translucency and privacy to the subsequent offices. The atrium had to be modified to accommodate a large dealing room. A new floor was introduced, splitting the original space. The marble floor with a central pond provides a focus to the executive reception area.

ARCHITECT: David Turner, Jane Rhodes, Sam Bayne and Alex Redgrave for Business Design Group, London, England

The Meiko Building, Aztec West Business Park, Bristol, Avon, England
Strong geometrical figures are shadowed in a floor pattern; illumination comes from carefully engineered ceiling lighting systems which emphasizes the contrast set up by soft fabrics and natural materials.
ARCHITECT: Tracey Wylde and Judith Rainford for Business Design Group, London, England

AT&T Building, London, England
An internal lobby space places a heavy burden
on artificial lighting. At the AT&T's
Communication Planning Centre, task, spot and
ambient lighting systems have been composed
to great effect. The main reception, a study in
understated elegance, welcomes guests, and an
obvious passageway is created by the curved
corridor that leads visitors through to the
secondary reception.
ARCHITECT: Jane Rhodes, Yvonne
Hollingsworth, Andrew Ramsey and John
Taylor for Business Design Group,
London, England

Bank of China, Hong Kong

The principal lobby to the banking hall has clearly expressed the geography of the building. To amplify the route from the ground plane, a huge kite-shaped void has been quarried out of the ceiling as a focus for the elevator. Polished stone exaggerates the precise internal geometries and floor lighting encourages direction.

ARCHITECT: Pei Cobb Freed & Partners, New York City, New York, USA

Bank of China continued over page

Bank of China, Hong Kong

Due to a critical shortage of land and a very small site, the requirement of the brief called for a tall building. In a dense urban environment it is often difficult to resolve issues of daylight and sunlight as a means of providing visual comfort to the internal office areas. Deep canyons have been quarried out into which light drops from above as the building steps back. The drama of the organizing void and reflected light ameliorates, to a degree, the problems caused by the building being remote from the outside world.

ARCHITECT: Pei Cobb Freed & Partners, New York City, New York, USA

IBM, Somers, New York, USA

The challenge was to build a large rural office facility in a way that would enhance rather than overpower the hilltop site. The solution was a campus-like grouping or a family of buildings: four interconnected offices organized round a nodal central services building. Skylit atvia penetrate the five main structures to create lobbies and points of orientation. The smaller office buildings are crowned by partial pyramids and the central block by a full pyramid atop the main reception area.

ARCHITECT: Pei Cobb Freed & Partners, New York City, New York, USA

Creative Artists Agency, Beverly Hills, California, USA

Interior activities visually spill outside via a monumental glazed entrance which also allows a large Lichtenstein painting to be enjoyed from the street. The transparent entrance establishes an inviting public image for the headquarters of this prominent literary and talent agency. Day and night it reveals the passage of agents and clients across the atrium in cinematic fashion. The atrium was designed as both a formal reception hall and as the operational core of the building. The radiating skylight screened by polished aluminium rods, provides controlled daylight and develops the building's radial organization through inflections of geometry and scale.

ARCHITECT: Pei Cobb Freed & Partners, New York City, New York, USA

Office Pavilion, Boston, Massachusetts, USA
The staircase to the entrance foyer and reception
area doubles to provide support for a number of
display units, creating another layer of texture to
a rich and colourful sequence of planes and
spaces.
ARCHITECT: Jung/Brannen, Boston,
Massachusetts, USA

Design Museum, London, England
Toplighting and filtered sidelighting variously
magnify and illuminate floor and wall surfaces to
create accents in the monochromatic interior.
ARCHITECT: Conran Roche, London, England

Truman's Brewery Building, London, England
The lobby leans against the principal section of
the building and captures a small garden. The
structure casts shadows to animate the floor
plane.
ARCHITECT: Arup Associates, London, England

Shonandai Cultural Centre, Fujisawa, Japan

Gridded glazed walls, exposed reinforced
concrete and a modest floorscape comprise a
utilitarian Lobby to the Cultural Centre. At night
the illuminated gridded glazed screens create a
cubic patterning of abstract figures.

ARCHITECT: Itsuko Hasegawa, Tokyo, Japan

The Tokyo Tepia Building
Careful detailing and a skilful orchestration of
natural and artificial light provides a calm and
passive lobby to this Japanese Cultural Centre.
ARCHITECT: Fumihiko Maki & Associates,
Tokyo, Japan

Tokyo Arts Centre, Tokyo, Japan
Fine structural steel detailing combines with
simple wall planes and a skylight animate the
atrium of the Tokyo Arts Centre.
ARCHITECT: Fumihiko Maki & Associates,
Tokyo, Japan

The Clore Gallery Extension, Tate Gallery, London, England

A staircase rises out of the entrance lobby directed by a glazed canopy to give access to a sequence of galleries.

ARCHITECT: Stirling, Wilford & Associates, London, England

**The Michigan Concrete Institute of America
Building, Detroit, Michigan, USA**
The central corridor focuses on a huge window.
It carries light along reflective floor and ceiling
finishes to provide a counterpoint to the
unfurnished wallings.
ARCHITECT: Minoru Yamasaki

Ford Foundation Building, New York City, New York, USA

The lobby, which rises to a huge rooflight, provides for an internal garden around which are arranged a number of galleries giving access to the administration offices.

ARCHITECT: Roche Dinkeloo, Hamden, Connecticut, USA

Daido Grove Plaza, Taipei, Taiwan
A sloping glazed roof covers the lobby and
provides light for the rich internal landscape.
ARCHITECT: Takenaka Komuten Co Ltd,
Tokyo, Japan

Hong Kong & Shanghai Bank, Hong Kong
The building's primary structural system is
exposed to the central atrium space to provide
scale, articulation and monumentality to one of
the world's great banking buildings.
ARCHITECT: Foster Associates, London, England

Chicago Board of Trade Addition, Chicago, Illinois, USA
The glazed canopy over the huge central atrium casts shadows against the multi-layered interior. The relationship of glazing patterns, lift shafts and cladding systems provide further visual interest to the heroic scale of the interior.
ARCHITECT: Murphy/Jahn, Chicago, Illinois, USA

3 East 45th Street, New York City, New York, USA

This 20 year old lobby was renovated by replanning the space into a forced perspective accentuated by a mirrored ceiling that reflects the marbled floor. Neon cut-outs beside and above elevator doors indicate floor destination and car use. An accent wall of hand-tooled pink lessinia stone, topped with a caged cold cathode fixture adds contrasting texture to the overall warm envelope. Polished brass add lustre to the elevator doors and wall panels as well as the custom-designed building directory.

ARCHITECT: Bromley Jacobsen, New York City, New York, USA

Runkel Hue Williams Gallery, London, England
The entrance way is distinguished by its minimal simplicity which, with careful use of light, provides drama in a surprisingly small space.
ARCHITECT: Pawson Silvestrin, London, England

Mississauga City Hall, Toronto, Ontario, Canada

The lobby is toplit with surrounding walls marked out with patterns of internal windows to provide a space reminiscent of the Ital,ian Piazza. The scale of the atrium area is relatively intimate compared to the monumentality of the staircase.

ARCHITECT: Jones & Kirkland, Toronto, Ontario, Canada

The Grianan Building, Dundee, Scotland
A light steel bridge unites two parts of the
building's composition. The rough stone-walling
recalls the archaeology of the undeveloped site
while the light, tubular steel and glass framing is
an icon of modern industrial building
technology. The lobby arbitrates between these
contrasts, bringing them together in a void
through space and light.
ARCHITECT: Nicoll Russell Studios, Dundee,
Scotland

Repertory Theatre, Dundee, Scotland
The main foyer is articulated by a huge wall of glass, through which the reflection of the auditorium can be seen in a stepped, ramped ceiling which acts as a canopy over the bars and restaurant areas.

ARCHITECT: Nicoll Russell Studios, Dundee, Scotland

Industrial Kitchen, Paris, France
Within a narrow cut in the building's fabric, topped by a glass canopy, industrial sidings reflect either side of a narrow staircase to create a lobby of extraordinary drama and presence for a building of such utilitarian function.
ARCHITECT: Philippe Gazeau, Paris, France

Delaney, Fletcher, Slaymaker, Delaney, Bozell, London, England

The lobby area for the merged offices of two advertising agencies is dominated by a long, glazed illuminated desk which marks the turning point of the space; this is reinforced by a change of materials, colour and texture. The two aspects of the company's activities are given literal expression in the scheme by the creation of two walls, one curving and sheathed in vertical oak plank, the other straight and tiled in electric blue glass mosaic. The walls come together in the reception area, where the laconic treatment of the other surfaces emphasize their significance.

ARCHITECT: Harper MacKay, London, England

The Reader Newspaper, Chicago, Illinois, USA
Stepped diagonals, gridded glass frames and a cubic composition of posts and beams mark out this lobby with a clear and precise geometrical discipline. It is part of a six-storey loft conversion which houses a local newspaper and commercial office space.
ARCHITECT: Pappageorge Haymes, Chicago, Illinois, USA

Roppongi Prince Hotel, Tokyo, Japan

Kurokawa describes the vertical circulation in the lower lobby to the upper areas as 'the Escher staircase'. The step diagonal of the real stair is reflected in a stepped frieze that implies a continuation of circulation both on the horizontal and the vertical planes. The hotel was designed to serve as a salon, and the central courtyard is occupied by a swimming pool, heated terrace, coffee shops and restaurants.

ARCHITECT: Kisho Kurakawa, Tokyo, Japan

Apple Computers Headquarters, Stockley Park, Heathrow, London, England
A light steel staircase rises from a huge carpet of beech flooring surrounding a collection of trees to physically and visually connect the lower floors to the upper levels.
ARCHITECT: Troughton McAslan, London, England

Citibank, Long Island, New York, USA
Exposing the huge skeletal structure of the
building as a component of the interior is
appropriate for lobbies on the grand scale.
During the day, light floods through the internal
spaces and soaks into the highly polished large
scaled floor to give extra colour.
ARCHITECT: Skidmore, Owings & Merrill,
New York City, New York, USA

Wacoal Kojimachi Building, Tokyo, Japan

The Wacoal Company design and manufacture
lingerie, and needed a multivalent space in their
new building to simultaneously fulfil a variety of
functions from product design via display to
warehousing. The entrance hall is a windowless
space bounded by stone wall panels lit from
above by lights grouped in threes, creating a
formal composition. The lobby is toplit, with the
steel and glass structure being reflected in a floor
pattern below.

ARCHITECT: Kisho Kurakawa, Tokyo, Japan

Offices of T. L. Horton, Dallas, Texas, USA
Bright red balustrades mark out the powerful
horizontal line of a raised balcony and the
stepped diagonal of the principal staircase tha6t
rises from the lobby to the upper floors. With the
exception of furniture and framings, all the other
surfaces are monochromatic to form a light and
passive envelope.
ARCHITECT: T. L. Horton, Dallas, Texas, USA

Municipal Nursery, Paris, France
An external wall and an internal screen collide to mark one corner of an elegantly articulated lobby space.
ARCHITECT: Marc Beri, Phillippe Gazeau, Paris, France

Fukuoka Seaside Momochi, Sawara, Fukuoka, Japan

The Fukuoka project was planned to house banking and retailing facilities, at the same time retaining a local landmark identity. The cone-shaped atrium of the banking lobby is animated by a rotunda sitting under a polygonal rooflight that casts shadows to create complex wall patterns.

ARCHITECT: Kisho Kurokawa, Tokyo, Japan

Howell Henry Chaldecott Lury, London, England

HHCL, a rising advertising agency, commissioned an 'office in the round', moulding space to reflect the way they do business. Work is seen to be being done; meeting rooms are approached through the body of the office; even the reception area is some distance from the main entrance. A copper and walnut panelled entrance lobby slices through the wall, giving an impression of a section through a solid mass. On arrival at the reception area, a serpentine, crown-cut elm counter nudges the visitor along a row of elliptical plaster columns in the direction of the horseshoe-shaped terrazzo and elm reception desk.

ARCHITECT: Harper Mackay, London, England

Columbia Studio Plaza, Burbank, California, USA

The building mass is articulated to bring the night sky into a formal architectural composition. Floor surfaces, lighting panels and balustrades take the eye on a predetermined conducted tour of the building. The pattern and colouration of the wood throughout the lobby and public areas echo the exterior finishes of warm-toned limestone.

ARCHITECT: Gensler Associates, San Francisco, California, USA

PHH, Windmill Business Park, Swindon, Wiltshire, England

The geometry of the lobby is reflected in the floor patterns, with the position of the reception desk being powerfully marked from above by the line base of the large white circular column. The overhanging gallery offers special security and a greater level of intimacy to the reception area. The reception is curved to create a more welcoming effect.

ARCHITECT: McColl, London, England

Stirling Hotel, Heathrow, London, England

The 4-star, 397 bedroom Stirling Hotel was commissioned by BAA Hotels Ltd. The white parallelogram shape reflects its airport location as a clearly articulated architectural statement. The huge central atrium is enclosed by bedroom ranges on either side. The lobby space, as well as being characterized by artworks and the white skeletal steel supporting structure, is lit by two glazed walls extending the full height and width of the end elevation.

ARCHITECT: Manser Associates, London, England

Aviation House, Gatwick, Surrey, England
The headquarters of the Civil Aviation Authority
is designed in steel, aluminium and tinted glass
to recall the sleek engineering of the
aeronautical tradition. A huge central atrium is
flanked by open plan office blocks and crossed
by bridges and lift towers. A close-up view of the
activities on Gatwick's main runway is possible
from all parts of the atrium.
ARCHITECT: Fitzroy Robinson, London, England

South East Bank, Miami, Florida, USA
The huge banking lobby comprises a structural canopy which acts as a shade net covering a forest of palms at plaza level, creating harmony and tension simultaneously.
ARCHITECT: Skidmore, Owings & Merrill

Harborside Financial Center, Jersey City, New Jersey, USA

An enormous old riverside warehouse was transformed into residential, retail and office space. The value of the waterfront was maximized by extending its presence further into the site. A redundant service court covered with a lightweight roof became the atrium, the primary entrance on the east side of the building. Glass and steel were used to offer a contrast to the heavy masonry of the existing building. The atrium is the heart of Harborside, a central focus for gatherings; planted with bamboo trees, it is a popular place for public events.

ARCHITECT: Beyer Blinder Belle, New York City, New York, USA

3i Building, London, England

Strong, dramatic architectural features create a focal point in the lobby area; visual interest is centred on the cherry-veneer reception desk. The combination of a stainless steel gantry suspension fixture, vibrant blue central pillar and sweeping curved staircase imparts a feeling of grandeur and success.

ARCHITECT: Peter Leonard Associates, London, England

The Ceresota Building, Minneapolis, Minnesota, USA

This historic 1908 grain elevator was converted into a contemporary office facility in accordance to strict historic guidelines. The exterior remains much the same as it was originally; within, the interior is organized round a huge mirrored atrium that opens to rooftop skylights. The new entry canopy and lobby structure is derived from a former train shed adjacent to the building; a masonry colannade marks the centre of the composition.

ARCHITECT: Ellerbe Becket, Minneapolis, Minnesota, USA

Hatton Garden Diamond Centre, London, England

The need for high-level security made the Diamond Bourse building appear antagonistic to the public and would-be lessees of the vacant office space. The solution was a reptile-like intervention, whose skeletal form both sheltered and announced the presence of the building on the street, replacing the old shopfront. Behind a curved glass façade, a cool metal canopy hangs above the granite floor of a large reception area. The hard quality of the street is continued into the interior; the reception desk resembles street furniture rather than the usual plush of a city office block. At night, the glazed façade allows the building's transparency to declare itself securely to the street.

ARCHITECT: ORMS, London, England

**Arthur's Quay Shopping Centre, Limerick,
County Limerick, Eire**
White circular section columns supports domed
rooflight over a large atrium area lit by pendant
lights and surrounded by black steel cross-
braced railings.
ARCHITECT: Crabtree Hall, London, England

The Lloyds Building, London, England
The proportions of the major space surrounded
by light layers of steelwork and visually tied
together by a complex of escalators create a
formal complexity within a very simple void.
ARCHITECT: Richard Rogers Partnership, London,
England

The Poynter Institute for Media Studies, St Petersburg, Florida, USA
The Institute was conceived as an encompassing landscape of outdoor rooms defined by, and interwoven with, inner spaces that focus on a skylit, two-storey atrium. This makes a Great Hall a dramatic public gathering spot, characterized by a forest of column beams and structural trees that support lightweight walls, and an enormous skylight that floods the interior with natural light. Floors and structure both reflect light to create a mellow richness.
ARCHITECT: Jung/Brannen Associates, Boston, Massachusetts, USA

Ove Arup & Partners, London, England
The central atrium is reminiscent of the small off-
street squares of Paris; a glazed canopy protects
the internal windows. White walls are washed by
high level lights to emphasize the relationship of
solid to void and produce by reflection an even,
ambient light.
ARCHITECT: Jestico + Whiles, London,
England

The Policy Studies Institute, London, England
A particular challenge was presented by the tapering wedge-shape of the light industrial 1920s host building. A small atrium unites the floors of the building, making the centre of the deep plan space usuable as a cellular office space and helping to resolve the problems of heating, lighting and ventilation. The triangular void is capped with a gridded glazed ceiling and amplifies the skeletal steel framing to the principal lobby space.
ARCHITECT: Jestico + Whiles, London, England

The Clove Building, Butler's Wharf, London, England

The Clove Building is a renovated converted warehouse adjacent to the Design Museum in London's Dockland. The main entrance is an entirely new structure containing lifts and stairs to serve each floor. A single linear flight leads from the ground floor reception to a first-floor gallery space. Selective demolition of the original building created a central light well bringing light into the deep plan spaces. The regular grid of the existing structure is abandoned on the top floor, where the wide spans of the new roof are supported on a minimum of slender, circular columns.

ARCHITECT: Allies and Morrison Architects, London, England

The Scott Howard Building, London, England
Built to replicate the exterior of St James church, which was considered structurally unsound and demolished in 1981, the Scott Howard building has a reconstructed façade of stucco and solid brickwork. The entrance is to one side of the classical elevation. The doorstep becomes a bridge through one of the brick arches which crosses a double height space between office and façade. The space is reiterated above, where the office floors open out onto a two-storey atrium.
ARCHITECT: Allies and Morrison, London, England

The Ministry of Social Welfare and Employment, The Hague, Netherlands

The spatial backbone of this low-level office complex is the hall which extends from one end of the building to the other across several storeys; it is the main artery where all communal facilities are located. Its street-like character is intensified by the glass roofs and the direct access to the terraces which are open to everyone. Social interaction is encouraged by this central zone, which removes the strict separation between different floors and thus spatially determines the entire internal organization.

ARCHITECT: Herman Hertzberger, Amsterdam, Netherlands

The T Building, Nakemagura, Japan
The main void that rises through the entrance
hall is distinguished by a galleried deck which
punctuates the void at midpoint. Strong colours
accentuate an abstract geometry that reinforces
direction to characterize a dynamic object in
space.
ARCHITECT: Toyo Ito, Tokyo, Japan

160

Waldron Allen Henry Thompson, London, England

A combination of patinized copper, translucent glass and differently figured timbers produces an engaging intimacy for this small lobby area to the offices of an advertising agency. A glass and steel staircase is planned, to connect reception with the lower floor through an elliptical lightwell.

ARCHITECT: Harper Mackay, London, England

Banking Project, Struer, Denmark

The main lobby has been designed to represent a street, with a line of standard lamps illuminating an upholstered bench facing a row of desks, like parked cars beside the kerb.

ARCHITECT: Bang & Olufsen, Struer, Denmark,

John F. Kennedy Library, Boston, Massachusetts, USA

The principal lobby is capped with a glazed canopy to light the principal and organizing void, which appears to be scalloped from the solid. Alternating courses of white stone facings and black glass carry the eye from floor to ceiling.
ARCHITECT: Pei Cobb Freed & Partners, New York City, New York, USA

The Architectural Museum, Frankfurt, Germany

The toplit central void to the principal lobby space contains within it another building, much like the principle of the Russian Dolls. The inner structure is in the form of a perforated screen that has light leak through the secondary and tertiary spaces. This device of layering the lobby both vertically and horizontally is best celebrated when observed in perspective.

ARCHITECT: O. M. Ungers, Berlin, Germany

Watson, Farley & Williams, London, England

This small lobby to a lawyer's office combines an engaging simplicity with a clear geometric articulation of planes and spaces. The largely monochromatic interior is highlighted with leather, chrome and timber and is washed with a high level of ambient lighting.

ARCHITECT: ORMS, London, England

55 Vandam Street, New York City, New York
USA

This lobby services both a warehouse block and an office tower via separate elevator systems. One objective was the visual identification of the lobby along the more trafficked avenues; a second was the formal resolution of the awkward configuration of the space. The lobby is formally organized around the axis that delineates the entry sequence between the exterior and the tower elevator. The floor plane of grey, gridded terrazzo following the new axis is reflected in the ceiling plane through a grid of stainless steel airplane cables and suspended incandescent lighting. A shallow plaster dome to the left of the entry draws immediate attention to the main axis and serve to unify the disparate elements of the lobby.

ARCHITECT: Fifield Piaker & Associates, New York City, New York, USA

Columbia Savings & Loan Bank, Beverly Hills, Los Angeles, California, USA
The passive and largely monochromatic lobby space is juxtaposed against the crashing geometries of an eccentric floorscape that relieves the symmetry and agitates an otherwise orderly space.
ARCHITECT: Skidmore Owings & Merrill, Los Angeles, California, USA

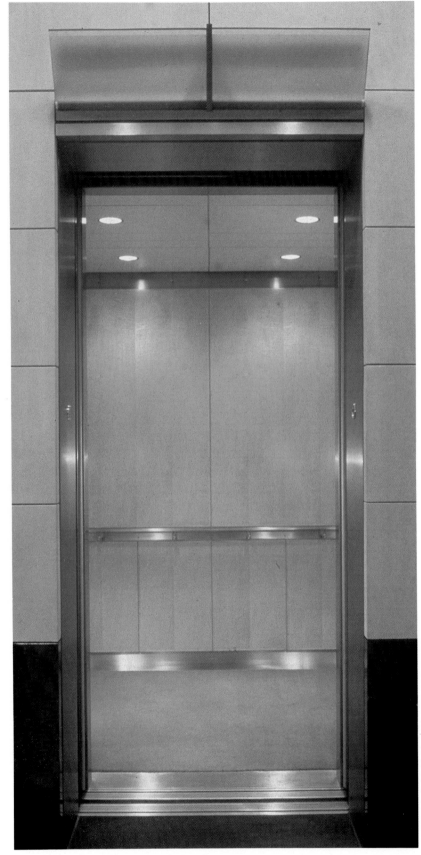

Foster Associates, London, England
The lobby to Norman Foster's London Offices is distinguished by the precise and articulate arrangement of a wide staircase as a simple stepped diagonal to intersect a cubic entrance void. The space is characterized by an elegant simplicity that relies on what is left out rather than what is kept in.
ARCHITECT: Foster Associates, London, England

New Modern

The closing of the nineteenth century was marked by a great explosion of creative activity. The enthusiasm for experiment, exploration and adventure carried the Arts into the twentieth century. The Americans were exploring various technologies for tall buildings, while Russia's imminent revolution promulgated the Suprematist and Constructivist movements; central Europe saw Wagner and Olbrich animate Vienna via the Secessionist movement, while Paris and Barcelona founded the *art nouveau*. In Great Britain, the Arts and Crafts movement foreshadowed Voysey's Modernism. Architects, artists, revolutionaries, writers and musicians came together to make a noisy proclamation of the spirit of the age and the optimism of a new time.

In the last decade of the last century of the second millenium, we should be recognizing and acknowledging a new wave of architectural expression that will develop its own characterization within the context of space travel, virtual reality, synthesizers, information and communication technologies and the ecological sciences. This is not to say that the new wave of architects and architecture will look like our perceived view of an aesthetic derived from twentieth-century phenomena. The new work captures the spirit of these contextual adventures, inverts it and abstracts it as an architectural metamorphosis of the emerging *zeitgeist.*

Like science, architecture has to experiment to proceed. It cannot go backwards without becoming the victim of sentiment; but without scholarship, nothing will have value or qualities. And without quality, nothing at all is worthwhile.

Louie Vega, Tarragona, Spain
The main entrance area rests under a lightweight canopy. The vaulted roof arbitrates between inside and outside, passing through the cloakroom, offering subtle quotations from Antoni Gaudí placed against the high technology of servicing and monitoring systems.
ARCHITECT: Alfredo Arribas Arquitectos Associados, Barcelona, Spain

Club Velvet, Barcelona, Spain

In common with many club entrances around the world, the lobby to Club Velvet is outside the front door. Unlike office and municipal buildings, club security takes place before the visitor enters rather than after. Emphasizing the *al fresco* place immediately in front of the entrance door of the club, the eyes of two steel doors peer down a suspended bridge that hovers over a dry moat of chippings. Lighting through a translucent floor serves to establish an exciting atmosphere in anticipation of the principal club areas beyond the door.

ARCHITECT: Alfredo Arribas Arquitectos Associados, Barcelona, Spain

Nave Rosa, Mercabarna, Barcelona, Spain
A glazed rotunda reveals and conceals a meeting room in the Nave Pastor complex. Lighting reinforces the texture of natural materials as well as highlighting the grain and figure of natural timber storage components.
ARCHITECT: Alfredo Arribas Arquitectos Associados, Barcelona, Spain

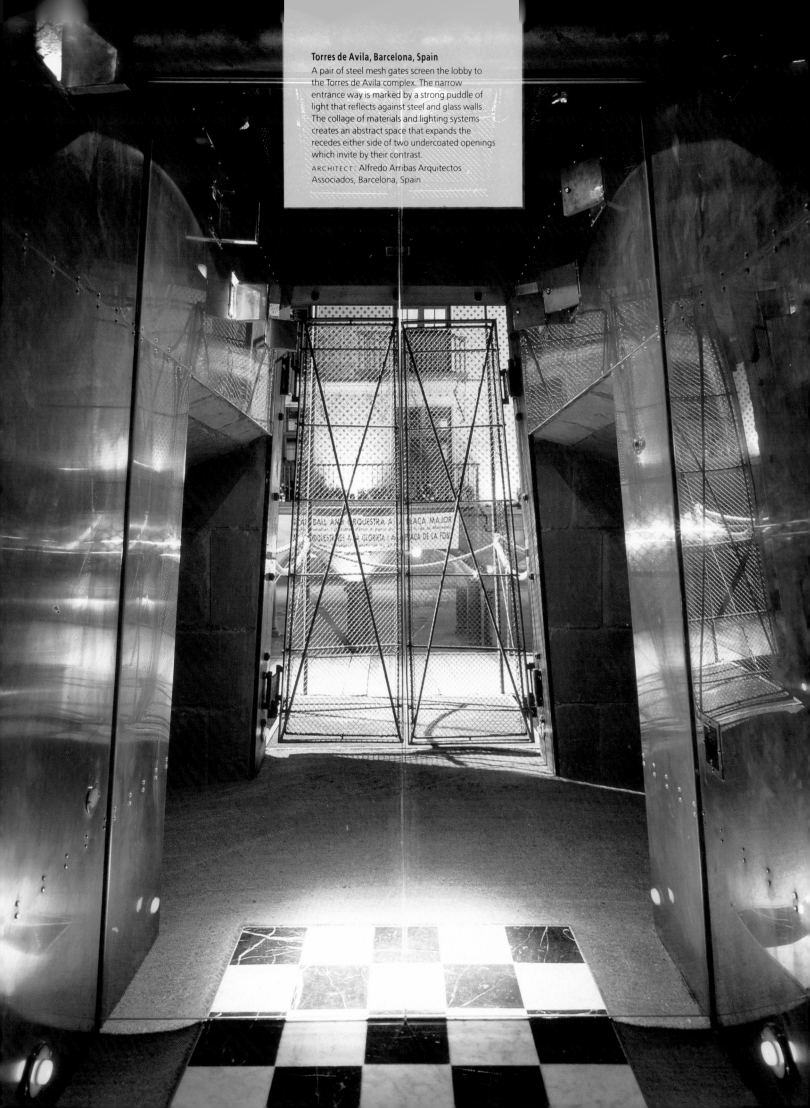

Torres de Avila, Barcelona, Spain
A pair of steel mesh gates screen the lobby to the Torres de Avila complex. The narrow entrance way is marked by a strong puddle of light that reflects against steel and glass walls. The collage of materials and lighting systems creates an abstract space that expands the recedes either side of two undercoated openings which invite by their contrast.
ARCHITECT: Alfredo Arribas Arquitectos Associados, Barcelona, Spain

**Ridgway Associates, Los Angeles,
California, USA**
The small lobby in L.A's Little Tokyo is a witty
collage of objects framed by an existing concrete
structure, glass block wall and simple white
reception desk.
ARCHITECT: Ridgway Associates,
Los Angeles, California, USA

Subterania, London, England
Subterania is a live music venue located beneath the elevated section of motorway, which acts as a canopy for an internal space. A steel framed gallery was constructed in the central part of this volume and the key facilities were arranged in a manner which emphasized both the presence of the concrete stanchions and the underside of the concrete slabs which form the motorway carriage.
ARCHITECT: Madigan & Donald, London, England

Origin I II III

Origin I, II and III are reinforced concrete frame buildings. Origin I has a composition of pink granite, black granite and concrete on the façade. Origin II is solely concrete. Origin III is made of black granite, concrete, aluminium and stainless steel. The lighting in the lobby is by standard recess lighting fixtures.
ARCHITECT: Shin Takamatsu Associates, Kyoto, Japan

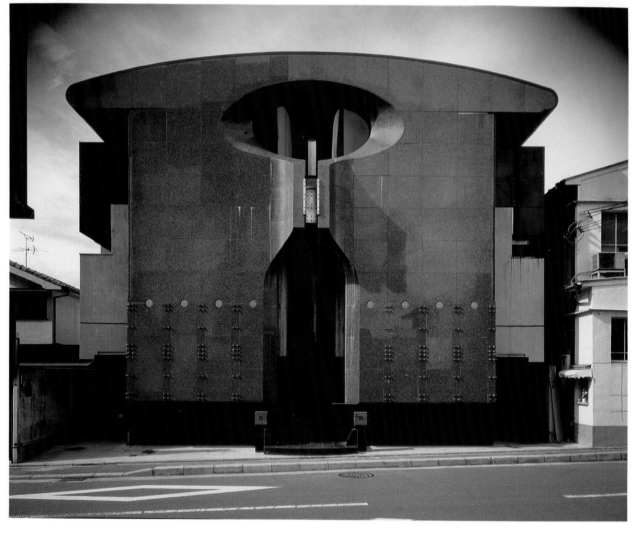

Atelier Baumann, Vienna, Austria
The lobby to this small atelier is marked by the
apparatus of the front door; eccentric steel work
supports a staircase and bridge that bisects the
principal space.
ARCHITECT: Coop Himmelblau, Vienna,
Austria

The Aerospace Museum, Los Angeles, California, USA
A powerful and often radical juxtaposition of structure lines, wall planes and spatial envelopes creates a canopy to the main lobby that is as dynamic as the building's function.
ARCHITECT: Frank O Gehry & Associates, Santa Monica, California, USA

215 Park Avenue, New York City, New York, USA

Essentially a long corridor, the lobby derives a spatial hierarchy through the interrelationship of barrel-vaulted areas, a precise palette of materials, and intersecting geometries. The vaulting is of brushed copper, lacquered to preserve its metallic sheen; walls are Indiana limestone with floors of solid black tipo marble. The continuous lighting cove provides direction and promotes sequence.

ARCHITECT: Fifield Piaker & Associates, New York City, New York, USA

The Kirin Building, Tokyo, Japan

The facade is composed of a mixture of black granite, aluminium and stainless steel. The four glass towers above are made from a composite material of rice paper sandwiched between two layers of glass. Each of the towers is lit on a two minute cycle and form passive elements against the multi-layered reflective surfaces of the lobby areas.

ARCHITECT: Shin Takamatsu Associates, Kyoto, Japan

Reception for WCRS/DMA, London, England

By setting up a relationship between baroque furniture and fittings, murals depicting pyramids and obelisks, radical textural changes and distorted planes, the designer has created a surreal lobby to the WCRS reception. The intention is to vary the decor with the seasons to reflect the mutable nature of the advertising industry.

ARCHITECT: Anthony Kawalski, London, England

Interventionist

Interior design has sometimes been defined as the art of creating new uses for old buildings. This is a specific definition which does not recognize the role of the designer in a number of other activities, including the provision of new interiors for new buildings or the creation of new uses for generic shell and core operations.

But within the re-use category, the architect has to persuade the host building to accommodate another function. The effectiveness of that persuasion depends on how good an acquaintance is made with the existing architecture. The architect must understand and establish a hierarchy of qualities in order to recognize the limit beyond which the host building would cease to be a benign partner in the marriage of new and old. The architect's job is to discover the essence or fundamental quality on which the building's character depends.

When this has been done, the interior design will become an intervention, a complete entity that is simultaneously recognized for its value as a part and its value with the host as a whole. The intervention will seek to enhance the qualities of the existing architecture and in so doing will itself be enhanced by the qualities of the host building. This architectural dialogue and dialectic can become radical. At its limit, it can create visual juxtapositions that are rich, dynamic and original.

The originality is usually most evident in the lobby, where new and old placed side by side within a major space make the greatest impact. Fifield Piaker & Associates in New York have exploited the potential for dynamic juxtaposition within the remodelled lobby for Gair 2, a warehouse transformed into an office building. At another level, Emilio Ambasz has only to twist a handrail eccentrically against the line of an historic staircase for the new to challenge the old.

Metropolis Recording Studios, London, England

The Metropolis Recording Studios were created by the conversion of a 19th-century industrial building in west London. The principal lobby space, which occupies the full height of the original building, is flooded with south light that drops onto a group of stairs and ramps, leading through a huge acoustic wall to the various recording facilities. Geometries are rotated and fractured in order to animate the entrance place and mark out the geography of the building.

ARCHITECT: Julian Powell-Tuck, London, England

Laings Club, Brighton, East Sussex, England
The building that houses Laings Club has space
for only a tiny lobby; instead of trying to enlarge
the space by using pale-coloured materials, the
walls are black and grey, in strong contrast to
the main club premises beyond. This transforms
the lobby into a dark, disorientating, excitingly
dangerous space; the feeling of potential
adventure is emphasized by fluorescent perspex
fittings which when lit through the floor transfer
light by table edges and the staves of entrance
totem poles.
ARCHITECT: Alan Phillips Associates,
Brighton, East Sussex, England

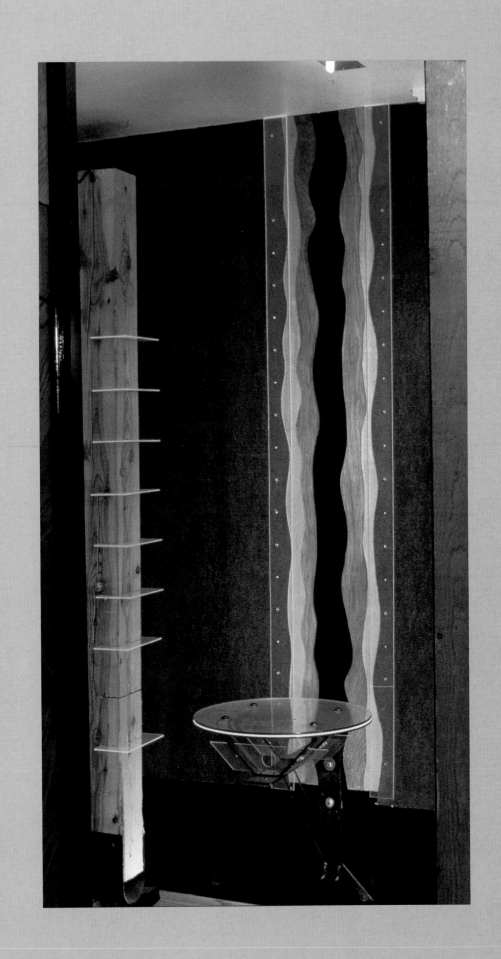

Visitors to
BROOKWOOD CHILD CARE

Proceed to Reception Desk on
4th floor.

Gair 2, New York City, New York, USA
The insertion of a new office lobby into an existing warehouse structure provided the opportunity to establish a counterpoint between old and new materials. Surfaces have been selectively sandblasted to expose their grain and figure; the hardness expressed by new materials provides a powerful contrast.
ARCHITECT: Fifield Piaker & Associates, New York City, New York, USA

Queensmead, London, UK

A transformation of 200 apartments in a development owned by the Norwich Union was brought about without radical expenditure on the architecture of the blocks. Instead, the public perception of the building was changed by relandscaping the gardens and lighting them at night, and restyling the entrances lifts and corridors. The intimate lobby is not resolved by a single geometry, but through a sequence of spaces that lead from and to a highlighted staircase and handrail.

ARCHITECT: ORMS, London, England

DEGW, London, England

The blue column is the only visible line of vertical structure in a composition of simple, elegant horizontals; a change of level is marked by a tall gridded glazed scrren.

ARCHITECT: DEGW, London, England

BMT Design, Chicago, Illinois, USA
This is the lobby to the offices and studio of the US toy industry's pre-eminent designers, and its creation called for an imagery evocative of the firm's purpose. First seen through a seamless glass storefront within the shell of an existing loft is a profusion of different coloured and textured fragments of support offices that establish the theme of a 'secret workshop' Visitors encounter spaces connected by a suspended model train and defined by iridescent glass panels and a backlit glass door. Gridded screens, cutouts, posts and a busy ceiling of exposed services combine to create an energetic lobby to a small building.
ARCHITECT: Pappageorge Haymes, Chicago, Illinois, USA

TSB Bank, St Andrew's, Fife, Scotland

A RIBA award winner in 1989, the TSB bank encourages a more inviting 'open-door' approach, endeavouring to bring banking back into the marketplace without sacrificing feelings of efficiency and care. The glass entrance screen, which slides almost magically aside through its split circular support is particularly welcoming; looking out, one still feels part of the street scene, the counters, with a refreshing absence of clutter being more like market stalls than intimidating barriers. Within, a group of gridded screens, stair planes and circular columns provide a horizontal and vertical layering of space from the ground to the upper floor of the banking lobby.

ARCHITECT: Nicoll Russell Studios, Dundee, Scotland

Exchange Tower, Harbour Exchange, London, England

The Harbour Exchange is surrounded by imposing architecture, and the brief was to create an environment that worked on a more human scale and was welcoming to everyone who entered. To create an immediate feeling of cohesion and familiarity, the layout is symmetrical. Both the reception area entrances and the main entrance lead the eye through to the circular fountain which provides a focal point. Graphic elements break up the formality of the layout. High curving glass panels carrying maritime images run through the mezzanine and ground levels dividing the reception atrium; outside, the main entrance is flanked by two huge vividly coloured banners which repeat the nautical theme.

ARCHITECT: Peter Leonard Associates, London, England

Goalen Group Office, Culver City, California, USA
This lobby space for the film design and production company locates inside a fractured rotunda, capped by a truncated conical roof window. The existing structural trusses are painted pale green to mark their new context among grey and brown plastered walls.
ARCHITECT: Eric Owen Moss, Culver City, California, USA

The Goalen Group Office continued over page

Scott Mednick Associates, Culver City, California, USA

The conceptual organizer of this project in a long central causeway anchored at the west end by an exercise room and at the east end by a stairwell. It follows an original line of wood post supports and correcting beams. Steel angles are bolted to both sides of the beams, aligned with lasers and shimmed to form a precise organizational reference line to which all additional components conform.

ARCHITECT: Eric Owen Moss, Culver City, California, USA

Scott Mednick Associates continued over page

**Hybrid Arts Qualitative Research Center,
Culver City, California, USA**
The conversion of a plastics factory offers an
opportunity to juxtapose a layering of painted
frames, arches and glazed panels against the
existing structure of timber posts and trusswork.
The intervention is seen as an architectural
palimpsest, where some elements have been
erased and some written over. The headquarters
of QRC within the overall project provided for a
specificity of intention to underline Moss's
powerful theoretical ambitions.
ARCHITECT: Eric Owen Moss, Culver City,
California, USA

Gary Group, Culver City, California, USA
This adventurous building for PR consultants has been designed, according to the architect, as a picaresque novel, that is a series of disparate adventures involving the same cast of characters. Like the novel, it can be opened and read at any point. Therefore, it has two entrances. One is cut from an almost free standing concrete block which rests on 'C' shaped steel nibs implanted in an adjoining wall. The second entrance is cut into a wall embellished with chains, wires, pipes, block planters and flowers. Inside the building, work stations are arranged within a cruciform plan. At the centre of the plan is a pool, open to the sky watered by steel shower heads which drop the water through a marble chute.
ARCHITECT: Eric Owen Moss, Culver City, California, USA

Index of Projects

A

Aarhus Town Hall, Aarhus, Denmark   17
The Aerospace Museum, Los Angeles, California, USA   188–9
Apple Computers Headquarters, London, England   131
The Arab World Institute, Paris, France   77
The Architectural Museum, Frankfurt Germany   166
Arthur's Quay, Limerick, County Limerick, Eire   149
Ove Arup & Partners, London, England   152
AT & T, London, England   96–7
AT & T Executive Communications Center, Woodbridge, New Jersey, USA   22
Aviation House, Gatwick, Surrey, England   141

B

Bang & Olufsen Banking Project   163
Bank of China, Hong Kong,   11, 98–100
Banque Bruxelles Lambert, Milan, Italy   20
Battery Park Financial Center, New York City, New York, USA   12. 36–7
Atelier Baumann, Vienna, Austria   186–7
Brussels Airport Sheraton, Brussels, Belgium   37
Beverly Wilshire Hotel (Regent), Beverly Hills, Los Angeles, California, USA   40
BMT Design, Chicago, Illinois, USA   206
Bond Street House, London, England   27
BP Headquarters, Hemel Hempstead, Hertfordshire, England   83
BUPA, Leicester, England   21
The Burrell Gallery, Glasgow, Scotland   68

C

Canada Life, Potters Bar, Hertfordshire, England   58–9
Capita Centre, Sydney, New South Wales, Australia   90–1
The Ceresota Building, Minneapolis, Minnesota, USA   146–7
Chicago Board of Trade, Chicago, Illinois, USA   116–7
Citibank, Long Island, New York, USA   132
The Clore Gallery, Tate Gallery, London, England   110
The Clove Building, Butlers' Wharf, London, England   154–5
Columbia Savings & Loan Bank, Beverly Hills, Los Angeles, USA   170–1
Columbia Studio Plaza, Burbank, California, USA   138
1133 Connecticut Avenue, Washington D.C., USA   43
Cook-Fort Worth Children's Hospital, Fort Worth, Dallas, Texas, USA   2, 24–5
Cour des Loges, Lyon, France   32
Creative Artists Agency, Beverly Hills, California, USA   102
Crown American Corporate Building, Johnston, Pennsylvania, USA   45

D

Daido Plaza, Taipei, Taiwan   113
John Darling Shopping Mall, Eastleigh, Hampshire, England   62
DEGW, London, England   205
Delaney, Fletcher, Slaymaker, Delaney, Bozell, London, England   128
The Design Museum, London, England   104
Disney World Dolphin Hotel, Lake Buena Vista, California, USA   48–9
Disney World Swan Hotel, Lake Buena Vista, California, USA   28–31
Dundee Repertory Theatre, Dundee, Scotland   124–5

E

3 East 45th Street, New York City, New York, USA   118
132 East Delaware Place, Chicago, Illinois, USA   36
Epworth House Securities, London, England   26
Executive Communications Center, AT & T, Woodbridge, New Jersey, USA   22

F

Farnborough Technical College, Farnborough, Hampshire, England   64–5
The Richard Feigen Gallery, New York City, New York, USA   74
Finlandia Hall, Helsinki, Finland   14
First Winthrop Bank, New York City, New York, USA   23
Foster Associates, London, England   172
The Ford Foundation, New York City, New York, USA   112
Four Seasons Hotel, Chicago, Illinois, USA   51
Four Seasons Hotel, Toronto, Ontario, Canada   41
Frankfurt Architectural Museum, Frankfurt, Germany   166
Frankfurt Museum of Modern Art, Frankfurt, Germany   80–1
Fukuoka Seaside Mamochi, Fukuoka, Japan   136

G

Gair 2, New York City, New York, USA   202–3
The Gary Group, Culver City, California, USA   220–1
The Goalen Group, Culver City, California, USA   210–213
Grand Hyatt Hotel, Hong Kong   50
La Grande Arche, Paris, France   69
The Grianan Building, Dundee, Scotland   122–3

H

Harborside Financial Center, Jersey City, New Jersey, USA   143
The Harbour Exchange, London, England   208–9
Hatton Garden Diamond Centre, London, England   148
The High Museum of Art, Atlanta, Georgia, USA   82
Hoare Govett Building, London, England   92–3
Hong Kong and Shanghai Bank, Hong Kong   114–5
T.L. Horton, Dallas, Texas, USA   134
Howell Henry Chaldecott Lury, London, England   137
The Humana Building, Louisville, Kentucky, USA   52–3
Hybrid Arts Qualitative Research Center, Culver City, California, USA   218–9

I

IBM, Somers, New York, USA   101
Industrial Kitchen, Paris, France   126–7
ITN, London, England   173

J

Jewish Community Center, Trenton, New Jersey, USA   16
JFK Center, Boston, Massachusetts, USA   73
JFK Library, Boston, Massachusetts, USA   164–5

K

The Kirin Building, Tokyo, Japan   192–3

L

Laings Club, Brighton, East Sussex, England   200–1
Lansdowne House, London, England   46–7
222 North Lasalle, Chicago, Illinois, USA   33
The Lloyds Building, London, England   9, 150
The Louvre, Paris, France   78–9

M

The Meiko Building, Aztec Business Park, Bristol, Avon, England   94–5
Metropolis Recording Studios, London, England   198–9
Metropolitan Square, St Louis, Missouri, USA   44
Michigan Concrete Institute, Detroit, Michigan, USA   111
Mineworkers' Union Building, Berlin, Germany   15
Ministry of Social Welfare and Employment, The Hague, Netherlands   158–9
Mississauga City Hall, Mississauga, Toronto, Ontario, Canada   120–1
Municipal Nursery, Paris, France   135
Museum of Modern Art, Frankfurt, Germany   80–1

N

Nave Rosa, Mercabarna, Barcelona, Spain   179
Neue Pinakothek, Munich, Germany   76
222 North Lasalle, Chicago, Illinois, USA   33

O

Office Pavilion, Boston, Massachusetts, USA   103
Origins I II III, Tokyo, Japan   184–5

P

215 Park Avenue, New York City, New York, USA   190–1
PHH, Windmill Business Park, Swindon, Wiltshire, England   139
Police Training Centre, Netley, Hampshire, England   66
Policy Studies Institute, London, England   153
The Poynter Institute, St Petersburg, Florida, USA   151

Q

Queensmead, London, England   204

R

The Reader Newspaper Building, Chicago, Illinois, USA   129
Regent Beverly Wilshire, Beverly Hills, California, USA   40
Ridgway Associates, Los Angeles, California, USA   181
Riverside Centre, Brisbane, NSW, Australia   10, 86–7
Roppongi Prince Hotel, Tokyo, Japan   130
Runkel Hue Williams Gallery, London, England   119

S

Santa Barbara County Courthouse, Santa Barbara, California, USA   61
The Scott Howard Building, London, England   156–7
Scott Mednick Associates, Culver City, California, USA   214–8
Security Pacific Hoare Govett Building, London, England   92–3

Sheraton Hotel, Brussels Airport, Brussels, Belgium 37
The Schlumberger Research Institute, Cambridge, England 75
The Schomerhaus, Vienna, Austria 70–2
The Shell Building, Melbourne, Victoria, Australia 88–9
Shonandai Cultural Centre, Tokyo, Japan 106–7
Sonesta Beach Hotel, Florida, USA 38–9
South East Bank, Miami, Florida, USA 142
Die Staatsgalerie, Stuttgart, Germany 8, 84–5
Stirling Hotel, Heathrow, London, England 140
Stockley Park, Heathrow, London, England 13
Subterania, London, England 182–3

T

T Building, Tokyo, Japan 160–1
3i Building, London, England 144–5
Tokyo Arts Centre, Tokyo, Japan 109
Tokyo Tepia, Tokyo, Japan,108
Torres de Avila, Barcelona, Spain 180

TSB Bank, St Andrews, Fife, Scotland 207
Tsukuba Civic Centre, Tokyo, Japan 60
Trumans, London, England 105

V

Club Velvet, Barcelona, Spain 178
Louie Vega, Tarragona, Spain 176–7
55 Vandam Street, New York City, New York, USA 168–9

W

Wacoal Kojimachi, Tokyo, Japan 133
Waldron Henry Allen Thompson, London, England 162
Washington Square, Chicago, Illinois, USA 42
Watson, Farley & Williams, London, England 167
WCRS/DMA, London, England 194–5
Windsor House, London, England 34–5
First Winthrop Bank, New York City, New York, USA 23

Directory of Practising Architects

This directory lists the addresses of architects in current practice. While every effort has been made to ensure that this list was correct at the time of going to press, subsequent changes in address or status are beyond the publishers' remit.

Allies & Morrison Architects
54 Newman Street, London WIP 3PG, England
PROJECTS: The Clove Building 154–5; The Scott Howard Building 156–7

Emilio Ambasz & Associates
636 Broadway, New York City, New York 10012, USA
PROJECTS: Banque Bruxelles Lambert Milan 20

Alfredo Arribas Arquitectos Associados
Balmes 345, 1 2, 08006 Barcelona, Spain
PROJECT: Nave Rosa 179; Torres de Avila 180; Club Velvet 178; Louie Vega 176–7

Arup Associates
2 Dean Street, London W1V 6QB, England
PROJECT: Trumans Brewery 105

Bang & Olufsen
Kjeldmarkvej 1, DK7600 Struer, Denmark
PROJECT: Banking project 163

Beyer Blinder Belle
41 East 11th Street, New York City, New York 100003, USA
PROJECT: Harborside Financial Center 143

Alexander, Freiherr von Branca
Obersohringerstrasse 167, 8000 Munich 81, Germany
PROJECT: Die Neue Pinakothek 76

Bromley Jacobsen
242 West 27th Street, New York City, New York 10001, USA
PROJECT: 3 East 45th Street 118

Business Design Group
24a St John Street, London EC1M 4AY, England
PROJECTS: AT & T 96–7; The Meiko Building 94–5; Security Pacific Hoare Govett 92–3

Chapman Taylor Partners
96 Kensington High Street, London W8 4SG, England
PROJECT: Lansdowne House 46–7

Conran Roche
Nutmeg House, 69 Gainsford Street, London SE1 2NY, England
PROJECT: Design Museum 104

Coop Himmelblau
Sellerstätte 16/11a, A 1010 Vienna, Austria
PROJECT: Atelier Baumann 186–7

Crabtree Hall Associates
70 Crabtree Lane, London SW6 6LT, England
PROJECT: Authur's Quay 149

DEGW
Porters North, 8 Crinian Street, London N1S 9SQ, England
PROJECT: Own Offices 205

Ellerbe Becket Inc.
1 Appletree Square, Minneapolis, Minnesota 55425, USA
PROJECT: The Ceresota Building 146–7

Fifield Piaker & Associates
72 Spring Street, New York City, New York 10012, USA
PROJECTS: Gair 2 202–3; 215 Park Avenue 190–1; 55 Vandam Street 168–9

Fitzroy Robinson Partnership
77 Portland Place, London W1N 4EP, England
PROJECT: Aviation House 141

Foster Associates
Riverside Three, Albert Wharf, 22 Heston Road, London SW11 4AN, England
PROJECTS: Own Offices 172; ITN 171; Hong Kong & Shanghai Bank 114–5; Stockley Park 13

Barry Gasson
Wardlaw Farm, Auchentiber, Ayrshire KA13 7RP, Scotland
PROJECT: The Burrell Collection 68

Phillippe Gazeau
17 rue Froment, 7501 Paris, France
PROJECTS: Industrial Kitchen 126–7; with Marc Beri: Municipal Nursery 135

Frank O. Gehry
1520 Cloverfield Boulevard, Santa Monica, California 90404, USA
PROJECT: Aerospace Museum 188–9

Gensler Associates
550 Kearney Street, San Francisco, California 94108, USA
PROJECT: Columbia Studio Plaza 138

Michael Graves Architect
341 Nassau Street, Princeton, New Jersey 08540, USA
PROJECTS: Crown Corporate Building 45; The Humana Building 52–3; Walt Disney World Dolphin Hotel 48–9; Walt Disney World Swan Hotel 28–31

Hampshire County Architects Department
Three Minsters House, 76 High Street, Winchester SO23 8UL, Hampshire, England
PROJECTS: John Darling Shopping Mall 62; Farnborough Technical College 64–5; Netley Police Training Centre 66

Harper Mackay
36–7 Charterhouse Square, London EC1M 6EA, England
PROJECTS: Delaney Fletcher Slaymaker Delaney Bozell 128; Howell Henry Chaldecott Lury 137; Waldron Allen Henry Thompson 162

Hellmuth Obata & Kassabaum
1831 Chestnut Street, St Louis, Missouri 63103, USA
PROJECT: Metropolitan Square 44

Herman Hertzberger
Vossiusstraat 3, 1071 CD Amsterdam, Netherlands
PROJECT: Ministry of Social Welfare 158–9

Hirsch/Bedner Associates
3216 Nebraska Avenue, Santa Monica, California 90404, USA
PROJECT: Grand Hyatt Hotel 40

Hans Hollein
Argentinierstrasse 36, Vienna 4, Austria
PROJECTS: Richard Feigen Gallery 74

Michael Hopkins & Partners
27 Broadley Terrace, London NW1 6LJ, England
PROJECT: The Schlumberger Research Institute 75

T.L. Horton Design Inc.
11120 Grader Street, Dallas, Texas 75238, USA
PROJECT: Own Offices 134

Arata Isozaki
6–14 Akasaka 9-chome, Minato-ku, Tokyo, Japan
PROJECT: Tsukuba Civic Centre 60

Jestico + Whiles Architects
14 Stephenson Way, London NW1 2HD, England
PROJECTS: Ove Arup & Partners 152; Policy Studies Institute 153

Jung Brannen Associates Inc
177 Milk Street, Boston, Massachusetts 02109, USA
PROJECTS: Office Pavilion 103; The Poynter Institute 151

Anthony Kawalski
14 Beverley Road, London W4 2PL, England
PROJECT: WCRS/DMA 194–5

Kisho Kurakawa Architect & Associates
11th Floor, Aoyama Building, 2–3 Kita Aoyama I-chome, Toshima-ku 170, Tokyo, Japan
PROJECTS: Roppongi Prince 130; Fukuoka Seaside Momochi 136; Wacoal Kojimachi 133

Peter Leonard Associates Ltd
55 Kings Road, London SW10 0SZ, England
PROJECTS: Harbour Exchange 208–9; 3i 144–5